ICONS

JAY-Z

BY BETH GOTTLIEB

Enslow PUBLISHING

Please visit our website, www.enslow.com.
For a free color catalog of all our high-quality books, call toll free 1-800-398-2504 or fax 1-877-980-4454.

Library of Congress Cataloging-in-Publication Data

Names: Gottlieb, Beth, author.
Title: Jay-Z / Beth Gottlieb.
Description: Buffalo, NY : Enslow Publishing, 2025. | Series: Icons | Includes index.
Identifiers: LCCN 2023059776 | ISBN 9781978540101 (library binding) | ISBN 9781978540095 (paperback) | ISBN 9781978540118 (ebook)
Subjects: LCSH: Jay-Z, 1969–Juvenile literature. | Rap musicians–United States–Biography–Juvenile literature.
Classification: LCC ML3930.J38 G69 2025 | DDC 782.421649092 [B]–dc23/eng/20231229
LC record available at https://lccn.loc.gov/2023059776

Portions of this work were originally authored by Roman P. Nacerous and published as *Jay-Z*. All new material in this edition is authored by Beth Gottlieb.

Published in 2025 by
Enslow Publishing
2544 Clinton Street
Buffalo, NY 14224

Designer: Tanya Dellaccio Keeney
Editor: Kristen Rajczak Nelson

Photo credits: Cover MediaPunch Inc/Alamy.com; p. 4 yuriyt/Shutterstock.com; p. 5 AFF/Alamy.com; p. 7 https://upload.wikimedia.org/wikipedia/commons/1/1d/Jay-Z%2C_Gloria_Carter.jpg; pp. 9, 11, 13 Featureflash Photo Agency/Shutterstock.com; p. 15 Everett Collection/Shutterstock.com; p. 17 WENN Rights Ltd/Alamy.com; p. 19 Suzan Moore/Alamy.com; p. 21 Brian Friedman/Shutterstock.com; p. 23 PA Images/Alamy.com;
p. 25 Abaca Press/Alamy.com; pp. 27, 29 ZUMA Press, Inc/Alamy.com.

Printed in the United States of America

CPSIA compliance information: Batch #CSENS25: For further information contact Enslow Publishing, at 1-800-398-2504.

Contents

Words in the glossary appear in **bold** the first time they are used in the text.

One of the Greats

In 2023, the Brooklyn Public Library held an exhibit, or show, honoring Jay-Z. Called "The Book of HOV," it included photos, awards, videos, and more. An exhibit like this shows Jay-Z's huge effect on music and **culture**. He's truly an **icon**!

The Book of HOV

ICONIC!

Over the years, Jay-Z's name has been written out Jay-Z, Jay Z, and JAY-Z.

Started from the Bottom

Shawn Corey Carter was born on December 4, 1969. He grew up in Brooklyn, New York, and lived mostly with his mom, Gloria. They lived in a poor neighborhood. It could be dangerous too.

ICONIC!

Many of Jay-Z's ***lyrics*** *are autobiographical, or about his life. Much of his early music was about the hard things he went through as a young person.*

Gloria

Jay-Z started rapping around age 9. He said it was easy for him! At first, people called him "Jazzy." He then changed his name to "Jay-Z." He and his friends started Roc-A-Fella Records to make their own music. Jay-Z's first album, *Reasonable Doubt*, came out in 1996.

ICONIC!

Reasonable Doubt *has sold more than a million copies in the United States. Many people see it as one of the best hip-hop albums ever.*

RADIO
MEGA
BLAST
Astros
abc

Another One

Jay-Z's next album, *In My Lifetime, Vol. 1* came out in 1997. Then, *Vol. 2 ... Hard Knock Life* hit number one on the charts! It came out in 1998. Jay-Z won a Grammy Award for it. He put out *Vol. 3 . . . The Life and Times of S. Carter* in 1999.

ICONIC!

Jay-Z doesn't usually write down his lyrics! He's said he has kept many songs in his head at a time.

On the Way Up

Jay-Z's albums continued to be hits. He put out *The Blueprint* in 2001. The song "03 Bonnie and Clyde" was on *The Blueprint 2: The Gift & the Curse.* It was Jay-Z's first time working with singer Beyoncé. *The Black Album* came out in 2003.

ICONIC!

Through the Shawn Carter ***Foundation***, *founded in 2002, Jay-Z helps kids who don't have a lot of money continue their education.*

Beyoncé

Retired?

In 2003, Jay-Z said he would retire, or stop making music. The next year he became the president of Def Jam, a record company. At Def Jam, Jay-Z helped young hip-hop artists. Rihanna was one of Jay-Z's new stars.

ICONIC!

Jay-Z wasn't retired for long. Kingdom Come *came out in 2006!*

A Big Year

Jay-Z was at the top of his game. He put out *American Gangster* in 2007. He stepped down as Def Jam's president that year. In 2008, Jay-Z co-founded the **entertainment** company Roc Nation, went on **tour** with Mary J. Blige, and married Beyoncé!

ICONIC!

Jay-Z was the first hip-hop headliner at the Glastonbury Festival in England in 2008 too! Before then, the music festival had only rock acts in the headlining, or top, spot of the lineup.

Working with Others

Blueprint 3, which came out in 2009, continued Jay-Z's string of successes. The song "Empire State of Mind," in which Jay-Z rapped about how he feels about New York City, featured Alicia Keys. It won the Grammy Award for best rap song!

Alicia Keys

ICONIC!

Jay-Z put out a book about his life so far in 2010 called Decoded.

Jay-Z is well known for working, or collaborating, with other hip-hop artists. He and Kanye West came out with an album together in 2011 called *Watch the Throne*. The pair won a Grammy Award for the song "Otis." In 2013, Jay-Z put out *Magna Carta Holy Grail*.

ICONIC!

As of 2023, Jay-Z had won 24 Grammy Awards total, tied with Kanye West for the most wins of any hip-hop artist.

The First

In 2017, the Songwriters Hall of Fame **inducted** Jay-Z. He was the first hip-hop artist to be honored in this way! That year, Jay-Z put out another album, called *4:44*. It featured personal lyrics that talked about his life and his marriage.

ICONIC!

Jay-Z and Beyoncé have three kids. Blue Ivy was born in 2012 and twins Rumi and Sir were born in 2017.

The Carters

Jay-Z's next big collaboration was with his wife! In 2018, he and Beyoncé put out an album together under the name The Carters. It was called *Everything Is Love*, and it won a Grammy Award! They went on tour together too.

ICONIC!

In 2019, Jay-Z helped found the REFORM Alliance, a group working toward positive changes in ***criminal justice****.*

Moneymaker

Jay-Z has long been known for more than his music. He co-founded the clothing company Rocawear. Roc Nation is a success, working with Rihanna, Shakira, and NBA star Kyrie Irving, among others. Additionally, Jay-Z co-owns TIDAL, a streaming service!

ICONIC!

In Kanye West's 2005 song "Diamonds from Sierra Leone" Jay-Z raps: "I'm not a businessman; I'm a business, man." Today, he's both!

Iconic

Jay-Z's induction into the Rock & Roll Hall of Fame in 2021 showed how iconic he is. President Barack Obama even spoke about the importance of Jay-Z's music in his life! Then, Jay-Z said in his speech: "Hopefully, I'm informing the next **generation** that anything is possible."

ICONIC!

Jay-Z took home the Dr. Dre Global Impact Award at the 2024 Grammys.

Timeline of Jay-Z's Albums

1996	*Reasonable Doubt*
1997	*In My Lifetime, Vol. 1*
1998	*Vol. 2 ... Hard Knock Life*
1999	*Vol. 3 ... Life and Times of S. Carter*
2000	*The Dynasty: Roc La Familia*
2001	*The Blueprint*
2002	*The Blueprint 2: The Gift & The Curse*
2003	*The Black Album*
2006	*Kingdom Come*
2007	*American Gangster*
2009	*The Blueprint 3*
2011	*Watch the Throne* (with Kanye West)
2013	*Magna Carta Holy Grail*
2017	*4:44*
2018	*Everything Is Love* (as The Carters with Beyoncé)

For More Information

BOOKS

Chang, Jeff, and Davey D. *Can't Stop Won't Stop: A Hip-Hop History*. New York, NY: Wednesday Books, 2021.

Smith, Elliott. *Black Achievements in Music: Celebrating Louis Armstrong, Beyoncé, and More*. Minneapolis, MN: Lerner Publications, 2024.

WEBSITES

Jay-Z Roc Nation
https://www.rocnation.com/music/jay-z/
Stay up-to-date on Jay-Z's music on the Roc Nation website.

Life + Times | Curated by Shawn "Jay-Z" Carter
https://lifeandtimes.com/
Explore Jay-Z's favorite music, fashion, and more on this website.

Publisher's note to educators and parents: Our editors have carefully reviewed these websites to ensure that they are suitable for students. Many websites change frequently, however, and we cannot guarantee that a site's future contents will continue to meet our high standards of quality and educational value. Be advised that students should be closely supervised whenever they access the internet.

Glossary

culture: The beliefs and ways of life of a group of people.

criminal justice: The ways laws are used to judge and punish those who have committed crimes.

entertainment: Having to do with interesting things people can watch or listen to.

foundation: A not-for-profit organization provided with funds to support charitable works.

generation: People born around the same time.

icon: A person who is very successful and admired.

induct: To officially list a person in a hall of fame or similar body.

lyrics: The words to a song.

tour: A trip to many places in order to play and sing music for people.

Index